Introducti

In this very small concentrated area of South
most beautiful waterfalls in the country. The
woodland at a low level, and as such they are ideally suited for wet days!
Many of these walks are also great for families or for those wanting a short
evening walk or quick excursion between showers.

The paths chosen are generally well trodden which, although great
for navigation, means that they often become very muddy in wet weather.
The rocks close to and around the falls can be extremely hazardous and
anyone venturing for a closer look needs to take great care and ensure that
their footing is secure. Some waterfalls require a deviation from the path to
see them. Again this needs great care as the views are often from balconies
perched high above the river. On hot summer days it can be very tempting
to have a swim in one of many deep pools encountered. But the water is
deep, often discoloured and usually cold. There are hidden undercut ledges
below water level and submerged debris such as trees which could trap and
hold you under. *So we do NOT recommend this.*

Although the paths are as a rule good, supportive footwear with a good
tread is needed. All the rivers in the area covered by this book respond
extremely quickly to rainfall, often with catastrophic flooding. Whilst all
may be well on a trodden path things can be very different if you are by the
water's edge and should happen to slip! So use your common sense, take
no risks, keep children under strict control and make sure you all return
home safely.

However, the lakes described are found in a much harsher environment
high up in the mountains (with some exceptions). Here you will need good
footwear, a map and a compass with, of course, the knowledge on how
to use them, and good weatherproof clothing. Always obtain a weather
forecast before you leave so that you know what to ecpect. If you fancy a
swim in any of the lakes bear in mind that the water will be very much
colder than at lower altitudes. And you will soon be out of your depth due
to the steeply shelving nature of these lakes. *Again we do NOT recommend
this.* Swimming in reservoirs is not allowed.

With all this in mind I am sure that you will really enjoy what this very
pretty part of Wales has to offer.

And if it rains, accept it – this will be the best time to see the 'plunging
water spectacle'.

LLYN Y FAN FACH

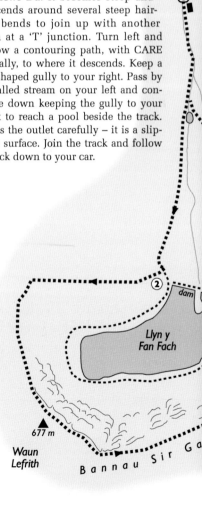

DESCRIPTION This pretty lake nestling under the dramatic cliffs of Picws Du has a wonderful legend associated with it. The walk can be curtailed at the lake by walking around it – 3 miles, or continued over Picws Du – 5 miles. This second option gives remarkable views from the grassy cliff edge looking down onto the lake. Allow 1½ hours if walking around the lake or 2½ hours if going over Picws Du.

START At a parking area by an information board beyond the tarmac road and Blaenau Farm.

DIRECTIONS From Llandovery turn up Waterloo Street where a sign indicates the way to Myddfai in 3 miles. Drive straight through Myddfai where a sign indicates the way to Llandeusnant. Continue to a cross roads with the Red Pig pub on your right. Go straight across here. There is a sign pointing the way to Llyn y Fan. Continue to a 'T' junction and turn left, again signed to Llyn y Fan. Where the road ends a stony track goes straight ahead with a sign again indicating the way to Llyn y Fan. Follow this bumpy track past a farm on your right to a where the track goes down right over a cattle grid and through a gate into a level area. Keep going to the information board.

1 From the car parking area walk up the track past the information board to some buildings and a locked gate. Turn left on a signed path and follow it to rejoin the track again. Follow this up to a track junction. Keep right and walk up to the dam. There are two options here. Either walk around the lake for an easy day and return the same way back to your car or – and this is much better – follow instruction 2:

2 From the lake bear right and follow a good, gradually ascending path away from the lake. *There are increasingly fine views down to the lake as height is gained.* The path levels when it reaches the broad ridge and then very gradually climbs over several undulations along the edge to the 749

metres high summit of Picws Du.

3 Leaving the summit the path descends, gradually at first but becoming very steep, to Bwlch Blaen-Twrch and a tiny stream. To your left, just before this, a narrow grassy path leads off. Follow this path under the cliffs of Picws Du. It becomes steep and descends around several steep hairpin bends to join up with another path at a 'T' junction. Turn left and follow a contouring path, with CARE initially, to where it descends. Keep a 'V' shaped gully to your right. Pass by a walled stream on your left and continue down keeping the gully to your right to reach a pool beside the track. Cross the outlet carefully – it is a slippery surface. Join the track and follow it back down to your car.

2

A **local young man**, the son of a widow from Blaen Sawdde near Llandeusnant, had agreed to marry a beautiful young maiden who had emerged from the lake. However, if he struck his wife three times she would disappear back into the lake. They were duly married. The maiden brought with her a dowry of some very special cattle that gave exceptionally fine milk. The couple remained very happy for many years in their house in Esgair Llaethdy, close to Myddfai, where they brought up a family. Over time the man did strike his wife three times, although unintentionally. According to the promise made the maiden disappeared back into the lake along with her cattle. On several occasions, though, she reappeared to help with the instruction of her children, especially Rhiwallon.

Llyn y Fan Fach

Eventually he and the other sons went to the court of Rhys Gryg from Deubarth becoming famous doctors who are known today as the 'Physicians of Myddfai'. Some of their medical formulas remain in Welsh manuscripts.

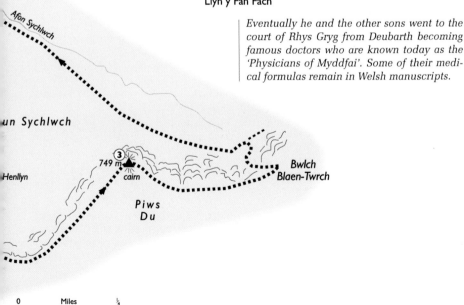

3

LLYN Y FAN FAWR

DESCRIPTION A fine 'lollipop' mountain walk or a there-and-back stroll. Llyn y Fan Fawr nestles under the steep ramparts of Fan Brycheiniog, the ascent of which is especially rewarding. There are spectacular views over the Black Mountain, the Brecon Beacons and down to the lake Allow 2 hours if walking to the lake and back or 4¼ hours if going over Fan Brycheiniog. *Note that in times of heavy rainfall the crossing of the Afon Tawe could be impassable, but then you wouldn't want to do this walk when you could not see the views!*

START At a parking area on the Trecastle to Tafarn y Garreg road by a wooden post indicating the right of way.
DIRECTIONS From Brecon follow the A40 towards Llandovery. On entering Trecastle turn left in front of The Castle Coaching Inn and follow the minor road, ignoring all the turnings, for 1½ miles to a 'Y' junction. Go left up the road signed to Abercraf and follow this, again ignoring all turnings. Drive through the Glasfynydd Forest and over the high point of the road. Continue 500 metres to the large lay-by on your right.

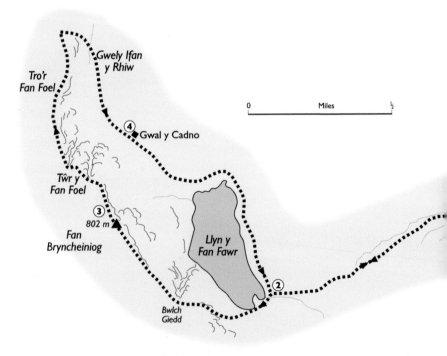

From the car parking area walk down on the well marked path, away from the pull in, to a tiny stream. Cross this and continue to join the infant Afon Tawe. Walk up the right hand bank of this passing several small, but very pretty, cascades in the tumbling stream to your left. The path crosses the Tawe above a small waterfall and continues gradually uphill, at times intermittently, to Llyn y Fan Fawr. Turn left at the junction with a more pronounced path and continue slightly uphill to pass a cairn on your left. Continue to the head of the lake. Either turn around here and retrace your steps back to your car or, much better –

4

2 From the head of the lake head towards the very prominent scar of a diagonal path on the steep hillside ahead. Follow this steep path up to Bwlch Giedd with increasingly good views of the lake. Bear right from the Bwlch before climbing a, thankfully short, steep path to the escarpment edge. Follow this easily to the 802 metres high summit of Fan Brycheiniog. *There is a fine circular wind break here and a trig point.*

3 Leaving the summit the path continues along the escarpment to a large cairn on the nose of Twr y Fan Foel with remarkable views of the lake. Keep following the escarpment edge to a circular feature with a stony circumference. Keep walking ahead to a well marked path that leads diagonally across the slope to the right. Follow this, descending Tro'r Fan Foel to Gwely Ifan y Rhiw and a faint 'crossroads' of paths. Turn right. The path very quickly becomes prominent but narrow. Follow this contouring path to the ruins of Gwal y Cadno.

4 Keep walking straight ahead here and climb up a short distance to where the path levels out. It then gradually descends to the lake shore. Walk around the northern end of the lake. A well marked path is then followed down the eastern shore to where you meet the path of your outward journey. Return by this route back to your car.

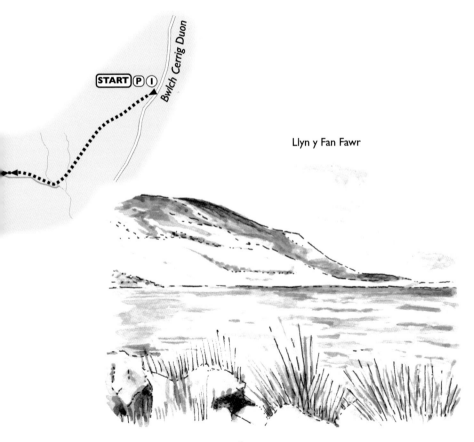

Llyn y Fan Fawr

HENRHYD WATERFALL

DESCRIPTION This 27 metres fall is the highest in South Wales. In high water conditions it is a splendid sight. The walk is only ¾ mile long but has a steep descent at the start and a steep climb to finish. Allow 45 minutes.

START At the National Trust car park near to Coelbren.

DIRECTIONS From the 'Heads of the Valleys' road – A465 – take the A4109 turn towards Glyn-nedd and Onllwyn. It is also signed to the National Show Caves complex of Dan yr Ogof. Continue to a cross roads and a set of traffic lights (the Dinas Hotel will be seen on the opposite side of the road). Go straight across and drive up the hill until a 'Y' junction is reached. Here the A4109 bears left. However, you drive the right branch of the 'Y' on the A4221 towards Abercraf. In a mile, at a cross roads, turn right where there is a sign indicating Coelbren and Henrhyd Waterfall. At the 'T' junction ahead turn right and at the next 'T' junction turn left up a narrow road. Cross the bridge over the Nant Llech and drive up to the small National Trust car park on your left.

L eave the car park by a gate next to the information board. Continue to the next gate 20 metres ahead and walk gradually down hill to where the path becomes much steeper. From the bottom of the slope bear left towards a footbridge. Cross this and climb wooden steps to the path that leads to the fall. On arrival you will notice a narrow path that leads off to go behind the fall. Follow this with CARE as it is very slippery. *There is also a great view of the fall from the waters edge.* To return, retrace your steps a short way until a path branches up to your left. Take this steeply to the top where there is a very convenient seat. Walk along the level path until it goes up slightly to a gate. Go through the gate to join the road and turn left. Follow the road to the 'T' junction. Turn left, cross the bridge and continue back to your car in the car park.

*I*n times of spate *Henrhyd is an awesome sight, but in summer it is a fine gossamer-thread-like fall. In these conditions the 'Farewell' rock is seen. It is fawn coloured and when the coal miners found this rock it meant the end of the coal seam. The fall is formed because of a fault in the underlying rock. A fracture crosses the stream at right angles to it which brings the coal measures up against the 'Farewell' rock. You will notice a shallow gully on the right of the falls marking the course of the fault and the face of the fracture. The highly polished and smooth vertical grooves are known as slickensides, evidence of vertical movement.*

In response to the increasing growth of the population and alarming and unthoughtful industrial planning the National Trust was formed in 1895. The lack of forethought by those early planners was beginning to threaten the beauty of the countryside. The Trust acquired the waterfall and surrounding woodland gradually between 1947 and 1965.

Henrhyd Waterfall

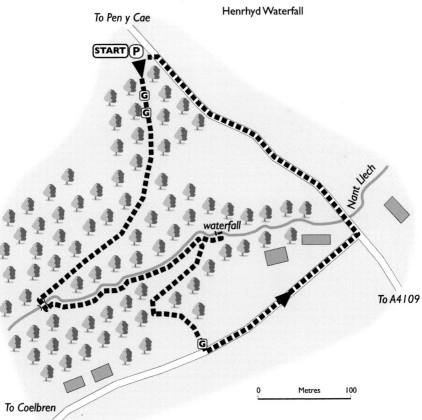

To Pen y Cae

START P

To Coelbren

To A4109

Nant Llech

waterfall

0   Metres   100

AROUND USK RESERVOIR

DESCRIPTION This is a pretty upland stretch of water at an altitude of 320 metres, much favoured by fishermen. Views from several places towards The Black Mountain are tremendous, along with distant views of the Brecon Beacons. An alternative to the main walk avoids some of the forest track that this follows. Allow 3 hours for the 6 miles circuit.

START From the car park at the east end of the dam.

DIRECTIONS From Brecon take the A40 towards Llandovery. Drive to Trecastle and turn left from the main road onto the minor road in front of the Trecastle Antiques building. Follow this road uphill at first and continue, ignoring all turnings, to a junction below the dam. Turn left – a sign indicating Usk Reservoir is seen at this point – and drive over the bridge. Continue up the hill, to the left of the dam, to the car parking area on your right.

I Walk from the car park up the road alongside the lake. The road deviates away from the lake to pass an Usk reservoir sign seen to your right by a track junction. Continue 300 metres further on the road to a junction with a forestry track going off to your right. This is marked clearly with two yellow topped green posts either side of the barrier. Follow this track. Ignore the junction to your right (signed 11 on your left) and walk to a left turn signed 12.

2 Follow this left hand track to the next junction – 13 – and bear right. Walk down and along the track to a 'T' junction and follow it to the head of the lake where a new footbridge avoids a ford! Keep walking along the track. It eventually joins another track. Bear right here. Continue along the track to a barrier and walk through the gate to the right of it. Continue along the track to the end of the dam. Walk across this back to your car.

ALTERNATIVE ROUTE

I Start as for the parent walk but only as far as the Usk Reservoir sign. Turn right and walk down the track and go through a gate to reach the lake shore. The next 50 metres are subject to flooding in very high water! Keep walking along the track to where it ends at the lake edge.

2 Go up to your left here and walk to the left of a fenced enclosure. From the end of the fence go up to your left on a path to a yellow topped post. Continue ahead with a fence to your right. Where the fence ends continue walking ahead to reach a hide. From this there are great views of The Black Mountain. Keep following the path to reach another yellow topped post. Bear right to a very muddy track and follow it up to a gravel track. Turn left and walk up to a right turning signed 12 (see above). Continue your walk as in **2** above.

The north-eastern edge of the reservoir (marked **A – B**) is wheelchair passable – with care. This in itself is scenic as it goes along the edge of the reservoir. It is 2 miles there and back.

The reservoir is the most recent one to be built in the National Park. Building started in 1950 and took 5 years. It was inaugurated by Her Majesty, the Queen on the 6th August 1955. The 478 metres long and 33 metres high dam holds back some 2,700,000,000 gallons of water. A supply tunnel 2,370 yards long goes under Mynydd Myddfai to the Swansea watershed where a 10 mile long pipe line goes to the Bryngwyn Treatment Works 2 miles south-east of Llandeilo.

Within the area there is a wide selection of flora and fauna. Red Kite are frequently seen and the Marsh Fritillary butterfly can be found here. The source of the River Usk is only a few miles upstream of the reservoir on Fan Foel. This reservoir has a reputation as one of the finest trout fisheries in Wales. The natural brown trout are supplemented by a regular restocking with rainbow trout.

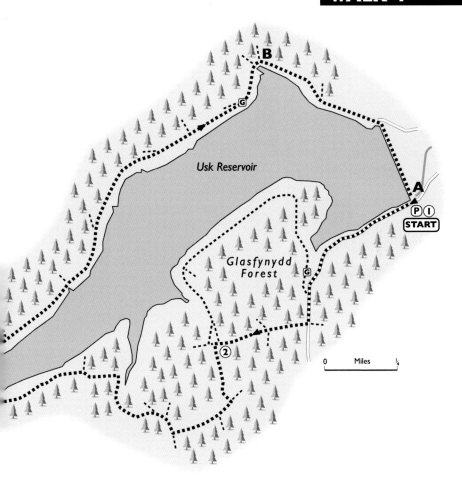

Usk Reservoir

Glasfynydd
Forest

START

0   Miles   ¼

About the author, Des Marshall

Des has had a lifelong interest in mountaineering, climbing, walking, canyoning and caving. As well as being an advisor, trainer and assessor in outdoor activities, he has undertaken many expeditions worldwide but recently focused more on local excursions. Having lived in Machynlleth for many years he now lives in Utah, USA, visiting Wales frequently.

SGWD GWLADUS, SGWD Y BEDOL (HORSESHOE FALLS), SGWD DDWLI ISAF & SGWD DDWLI UCHAF

DESCRIPTION Lovely woodland, pretty falls and mining history make this a great walk. Although 6¼ miles long, the walking is generally easy with just one steep section near the end. Allow 3 hours.

START At a small car park close to The Angel pub in Pontneddfechan.

DIRECTIONS From the 'Heads of the Valleys' road – A465 – take the A4109 turn towards Glyn-nedd and Onllwyn. It is also signed to the National Show Caves complex of Dan yr Ogof. Continue to a cross roads and a set of traffic lights (the Dinas Hotel is seen on the opposite side of the road). Turn right here and 300 metres further on turn left on the B4242 signed to Pontneddfechan. Continue to The Angel where there is parking close by. DO NOT park in the car park belonging to the pub.

I From the car park walk through the metal gate with Sgwd Gwladus clearly marked. Follow the good path to a gate and stile. Take your pick which you use! Continue following the track. There is evidence of mining along this section, as is evidenced by the blocked off adits. Continue to a footbridge. Do not cross this but continue up with the Afon Pyrddin to your right. *A viewing area is reached where Sgwd Gwladus is clearly seen.* Return to the bridge and cross over. Follow the Pyrddin upstream for an alternative view of the fall, then return to the bridge.

2 Do not cross but walk ahead to join the Nedd Fechan and follow this delightful river upstream. The path rises to end up high above the river but then gradually descends back to it again to cross a footbridge. Continue to the next footbridge where on the right is the lovely and well named Sgwd y Bedol (Horseshoe Falls). Continue upstream to above Sgwd Ddwli Isaf and another footbridge. Cross this and continue upstream to the next very pretty fall Sgwd Ddwli Uchaf. Here the approach to the bottom of the fall is via an easy path that leads off from the main path some 200 metres before the waterfall. Return to the main path and continue up to a picnic site at Pont Melin Fach.

3 Retrace your steps to a finger post indicating the way to the Silica Mine in 400 metres. Cross the bridge on your left spanning the Nedd Fechan and walk downstream passing a large opening on your left into the mine. DO NOT ENTER. Keep walking downstream to a stile. Cross this and pass by ruins on your left. These are unstable. DO NOT ENTER. Keep walking and cross a footbridge. Continue on the narrow path to a finger post and marker pole. The path now briefly doubles back on itself and zigzags up away from the river to a stile. Cross this and follow the path going slightly right keeping a fence to your right to reach another stile. Climb over this. Continue ahead passing several marker posts to a footbridge with a stile for access, and cross over. To your left 5 metres further on, climb over another stile. Continue across a short section of boggy ground to a stile to the right of the school. Climb over this and continue to reach the road.

4 Turn right along the road. Cross a side road and follow the signed path that starts just to the right of a bus shelter on a bend in the road. The path descends quite steeply and reaches a series of steps that are followed down to your car close to The Angel.

10

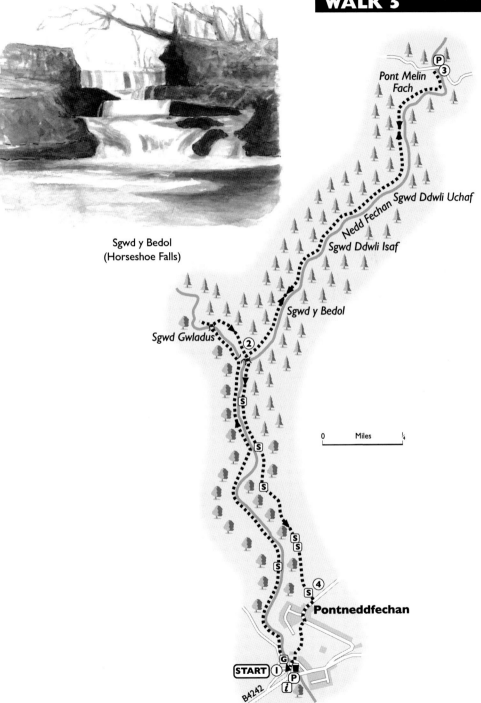

Pont Melin Fach

Sgwd Ddwli Uchaf

Nedd Fechan

Sgwd Ddwli Isaf

Sgwd y Bedol
(Horseshoe Falls)

Sgwd y Bedol

Sgwd Gwladus

0   Miles   ¼

Pontneddfechan

START

B4242

WALK 6

SGWD GWLADUS

DESCRIPTION Lovely woodland, pretty falls and mining history make this a great 2¾ mile walk. The walking is generally easy with just one steep section near the end. Allow 1½ hours.

START At a small car park close to The Angel in Pontneddfechan.

DIRECTIONS From the 'Heads of the Valleys' road – A465 – take the A4109 turn towards Glyn-nedd and Onllwyn. It is also signed to the National Show Caves complex of Dan yr Ogof. Continue to a cross roads and a set of traffic lights. (The Dinas Hotel is seen on the opposite side of the road). Turn right here and 300 metres further on turn left on the B4242 signed to Pontneddfechan. Continue to The Angel where there is parking close by. DO NOT park in the car park belonging to the pub.

I From the car park walk through the metal gate with Sgwd Gwladys clearly marked. Follow the good path to a gate and stile. Take your pick which you use! Continue following the track. There is evidence of mining along this section as is seen by the blocked off adits. Continue to a footbridge. Do not cross this but continue up with the Afon Pyrddin to your right. A viewing area is reached where Sgwd Gwladus is clearly seen. Return to the bridge and cross over. Follow the Pyrddin upstream for an alternative view of the fall and return to the bridge.

2 Ahead, spanning the Nedd Fechan, is another footbridge where a sign indicates the way to the Silica Mine in 400 metres. Cross this bridge and walk downstream passing a large opening on your left into the mine. DO NOT ENTER. Keep walking downstream to a stile. Cross this and pass by ruins on your left. These are unstable – DO NOT ENTER. Keep walking and cross over a footbridge. Continue on the narrow path to a finger post and marker pole. The path now briefly dou-

bles back on itself and zigzags up away from the river to a stile. Cross this and follow the path going slightly right keeping a fence to your right to reach another stile. Climb over this. Continue ahead passing several marker posts to a footbridge with a stile for access and cross over. To your left 5 metres further on, climb over another stile. Continue across a short section of boggy ground to a stile to the right of the school. Climb over this and continue to reach the road.

3 Turn right down the road. Cross a side road and follow the signed path that starts just to the right of a bus shelter on a bend of the road. The path descends quite steeply and reaches a series of steps that are followed down to your car close to The Angel.

F **or** an easier linear walk take the wide path just to the viewing area for Sgwd Gwladus and return the same way.

In the area around Pontneddfechan there are exposed beds of very hard and pure sandstone known as Silica rock. It was mined here from the late 18th century right up to 1964. The rock has very few impurities, being almost 100% silica. William Weston Young from the Vale of Neath developed a method of producing high quality firebricks from the Nedd Fechan and Dinas silica rock. Because of their high quality they were exported worldwide as well as being used locally to line furnaces in which iron and copper smelting took place. Only bricks made from the highest quality silica could withstand the intense heat without shattering. Today the Russian word for firebrick is 'Dinas'. The tramway up the Nedd Fechan now gives easy access to walkers where at one time horse drawn drams ferried the raw material to the early factory at Dinas Bridge. This was built by Messrs Frederick and Jenner. Later works were established at Pont Walby, Glyn-nedd. The largest of the mines was at Cwm Gored, which you pass by the ruins of the old works.

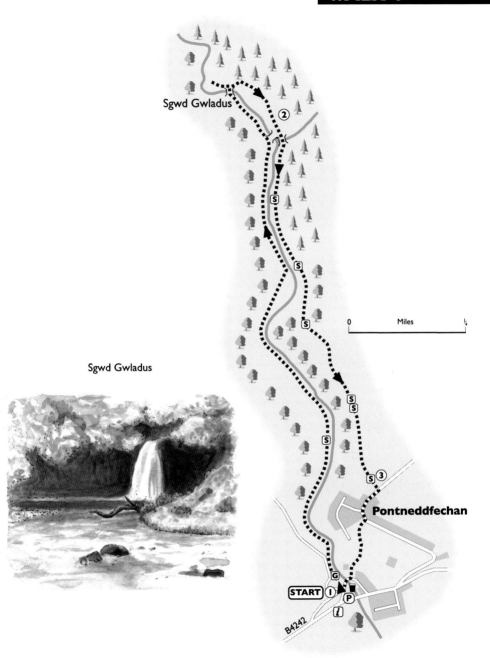

Sgwd Gwladus

Sgwd Gwladus

②

Pontneddfechan

START

B4242

0   Miles   ¼

WALK 7

SGWD DDWLI UCHAF, SGWD DDWLI ISAF, SGWD Y BEDOL
(HORSESHOE FALLS)
& SGWD GWLADUS

DESCRIPTION Lovely woodland, pretty falls and fine woods make this a great 3 mile walk. Allow 1¾ hours.

START At Pont Melin Fach.

DIRECTIONS From the 'Heads of the Valleys' road – A465 – take the A4109 turn towards Glyn-nedd and Onllwyn. It is also signed to the National Show Caves complex of Dan yr Ogof. Continue to a cross roads and a set of traffic lights. (The Dinas Hotel is seen on the opposite side of the road). Turn right here and 300 metres further on turn left on the B4242 signed to Pontneddfechan. Continue past The Angel to a 'Y' road junction. The Dinas Inn is on your right. Go left up the hill and around a steep bend. Continue through the village. Keep driving gradually uphill to where the road levels just past the well signed Gwern Blaedda farm. Turn left down a narrow road where a sign indicates that the road is not suitable for coaches! Follow the road down to the obvious picnic site by the bridge.

1 From the car park walk down the right hand side of the picnic site to join a path. Follow this to the first fall, Sgwd Ddwli Uchaf. Continue along the main path a further 200 metres. Turn sharp left to reach a wide trodden area by the river's edge. Follow this up to the fall. To continue the walk, return to the main path and follow it downstream to a footbridge near which is the Sgwd Ddwli Isaf. Cross the footbridge and keep walking downstream to another footbridge close to Sgwd y Bedol (Horseshoe Falls). The path continues downstream but ascends slightly to a point high above the Nedd Fechan before descending to a footbridge.

2 Do not cross this but continue upstream with the Afon Pyrddin on your left and walk up to Sgwd Gwladus. Return to the footbridge and continue back to your car at Pont Melin Fach.

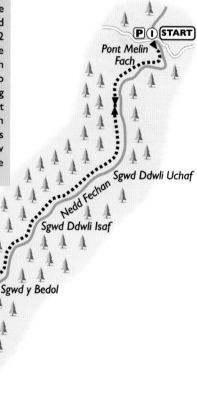

14

WALK 8

AFON SYCHRYD LOWER WATERFALL

all ability trail

DESCRIPTION Woodland, cliff scenery, pretty falls, mining history and industry make this an interesting trail. ½ mile, allow 30 minutes.

START From the car park at Craig y Dinas.

DIRECTIONS From the 'Heads of the Valleys' road – A465 – take the A4109 turn towards Glyn-nedd and Onllwyn. It is also signed to the National Show Caves complex of Dan yr Ogof. Continue to a cross roads and a set of traffic lights. (The Dinas Hotel is seen on the opposite side of the road). Turn right here and 300 metres further on turn left on the B4242 signed to Pontneddfechan. Continue past The Angel to where there is a 'Y' junction, the Dinas Inn is to your right. Bear right and continue to where the road goes right and crosses the narrow bridge spanning the Afon Mellte. Turn left at the far side into the spacious car parking area. Take a turning to your right into a parking bay complete with picnic table, a large boulder and a black and white post where the ramp access starts. PLEASE DO NOT PARK IN THE VILLAGE.

Go up the ramp that leads onto a gravel trail. This becomes somewhat muddy after heavy rainfall! Follow the trail upstream – with the river to your right – to a platform overlooking the waterfall. Note the fine natural folding on the roof of a natural cave at this point – Bwa Maen (stone arch) – on the far bank. Return the same way.

As you walk up the left side of the Afon Sychryd look out for some wavy rock features on your left. Opposite this on the far side of the river a keyhole shaped opening can be spotted. *This is an entrance into the Dinas Silca mines. Partially flooded they should NOT be entered. These mines were much larger than the ones by the side of the Afon Nedd Fechan. They were very extensive covering an area of some 1,000m by 500m. The material was transported by means of tramways, inclines and even aerial ropeways from the higher entrances down to the valley floor. From here it was transported to Pont Walby brickworks and in later years to Swansea until closure in the early 1960s.*

*T**here is a** legend relating to King Arthur associated with Craig-y-Dinas (Dinas Rock). It claims that the King is asleep under the rock waiting to rescue Wales from Saxon invaders. A story says that a Welshman from London visited the area and explored a cave under the rock. Here he found King Arthur with his Knights asleep inside. He was given permission to take the gold and silver from them but he had to remember to tell them to 'sleep on' when he left. On the first occasion he did but his greed took over on the second visit when he forgot, and became a ruined man*

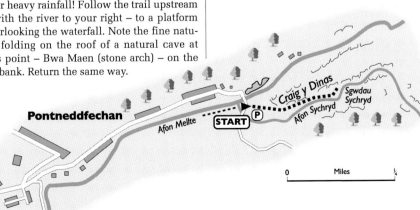

Pontneddfechan · Afon Mellte · START · Craig y Dinas · Afon Sychryd · Sgwdau Sychryd

0 ——— Miles ——— ¼

15

SGWD YR EIRA & UPPER SYCHRYD FALLS FROM PENDERYN

DESCRIPTION This walk visits one of the area's finest falls, Sgwd yr Eira (waterfall of snow) and continues through fine woodland to the Upper Sychryd Falls before returning to Penderyn via a gradually ascending path with great views of the Neath Valley.

START From Penderyn.

DIRECTIONS From the A465 'Heads of the Valleys' road take the A4059 road from Hirwaun towards Brecon into the village of Penderyn. Just beyond the Lamb Inn turn left and park close to the houses before the road bends to the right. *PLEASE DO NOT obstruct any driveways.*

I Walk straight ahead from your car along a good track which is signed to Sgwd yr Eira. Ignore the track on the left and continue to a kissing gate left of a larger gate. Go through this and walk along a level but muddier track ignoring the grassy track on the right. Follow the fence on your right to a marker post. Ignore the uphill track to your left and go right and ignore a stile to your right – marker post. Keep following the track up to where it deteriorates into a wide path. Follow this level path. It becomes very swampy. Continue to a two-step stile over a fence. Follow the fence up keeping it to your left to a stile on your left. Go over this and continue with the fence to your right, level at first and then downhill to a marker post where the fence goes off to your right. Walk left away from the fence and continue to a finger post and three way junction at some boulders. Go down to your right to Sgwd yr Eira. At first the path descends very gradu-ally then becomes very steep with steps. Continue around an acute left hand bend and down to the Afon Hepste and walk up to the waterfall which can be walked behind.

2 Return to the finger post and turn right towards Craig y Dinas. Continue along this path, which can be very wet at times, to some ruins. Bear right and down passing marker posts before bearing left along the main path. Keep going to a fence and a gate. Go through this keeping on the path to a finger post indicating the way to the Gunpowder Works. Ignore this and continue ahead to a fence. Turn left. Go down to where the path bends to the right with another going straight ahead. Bear right and continue down to where it descends steeply to reach a level platform overlooking the Afon Sychryd. The waterfalls are obvious, situated below a sturdy footbridge. At the far side of the bridge a large opening enters an abandoned Silica Mine. DO NOT ENTER.

3 Return to the path junction and turn up to your right. Ascend gradually, with increasingly fine views of the Neath Valley, to a gate. Go through this and continue ahead on the track to another gate. Go through this and follow the grassy track to another gate. Pass through this, and another, to join a narrow tarmac road. Follow this down to a road junction. Hirwaun is to the right, so continue straight ahead passing the Tafarn Llew. Continue down to where the road bends to the right. Go straight ahead back to your car.

W *ales' only whiskey distillery is situated on the outskirts of the village and is well worth a visit. The whiskey (you can only call it whisky without the 'e' if it is distilled in Scotland) is, not surprisingly, called 'Penderyn'.*

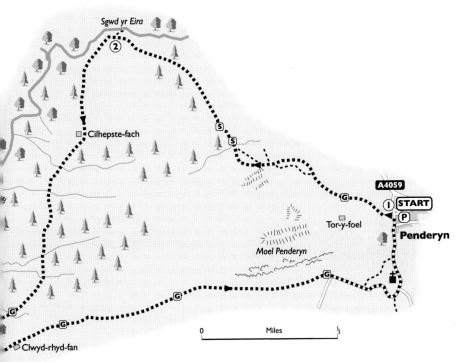

Sgwd yr Eira

AFON MELLTE & AFON HEPSTE WATERFALLS

DESCRIPTION This 4 mile walk visits many of the area's finest waterfalls: Sgwd Clun Gwyn, Sgwd Isaf Clun Gwyn, Sgwd y Pannwr and Sgwd yr Eira (waterfall of snow). There are fine river scenes and woodland. Allow 3 hours.

START From Cwm Porth Brecon Beacons National Park car park

DIRECTIONS From the A465 'Heads of the Valleys' road take the A4059 road from Hirwaun towards Brecon into the village of Penderyn. Continue on the road to a left turn signed to Ystradfellte. Follow this road to a 'Y' junction and bear left. Continue down this narrow road to a hidden junction on your left. Take this and drive down an even narrower road to the car park on your right.

I Cross the road from the car park and take the path that follows a short length of concrete causeway between two cave entrances. These lead into the Porth yr Ogof system. Bear left and follow the sign towards Blue Pool and Waterfalls. Go through a kissing gate and follow the path alongside the Afon Mellte to a footbridge. Walk past the bridge and continue on the main path up past a small section of fence on your left. Keep walking to join a fence to your right and continue to a finger post. Descend here to admire Sgwd Clun Gwyn.

2 Return to the finger post and follow the red indicator towards Sgwd yr Eira. Markers numbered 16 to 25 are followed to another finger post. To reach Sgwd yr Eira, continue to the next finger post – number 35 – pointing the way down to Sgwd yr Eira. Follow the path down via some steps to the

fall. It is possible to walk around the back of this. Return to the finger post and continue back to the finger post at point 25. Descend here to reach Sgwd y Pannwr by following markers 25 – 30. Walk upstream along the path by the river to view Sgwd Isaf Clun Gwyn. *IT IS RECOMMENDED that you return the same way to the finger post at point 25* and follow your outward walk back to your car in Cwm Porth.

ALTERNATIVE

2a For those who have a good head for heights, are experienced walkers and are sure footed there is another way back to the car park: ascend the steep tree root slope above the lowest part of Sgwd Isaf Clun Gwyn to join a very narrow and exposed path 30 metres above the waterfall. *Taking GREAT CARE, as a slip will inevitably be very serious,* follow this scenic narrow path below beetling overhangs to Sgwd Clun Gwyn. Walk up to the finger post and turn left. Return to the car park on the route walked on your outward journey.

__B__efore setting off for your walk a visit to see Porth yr Ogof is a 'must do'. Walk down the slippery path, with care, from the top left-hand edge of the car park to a seat at the bottom. To your left are twin stiles. Climb over either one down to the river's edge. Walk along a flat platform a few metres to its end. It is unwise to go further due to falling debris. The entrance, the largest in Wales, is 15 metres wide and 4 metres high. The river on your right is not the real river however. It is only an overflow from the main streamthat flows year round through the Tradesman's Entrance. This is seen by going to the right from the seat. Afon Mellte means 'lightning river'. It rises incredibly quickly during rainfall and goes down just as quick. There are 15 entrances into the system. Although used by many Outdoor Centres the cave has claimed the lives of 11 people.

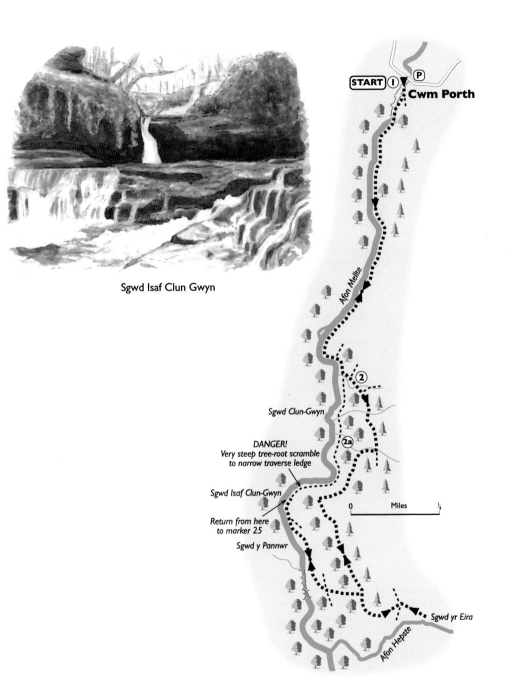

Sgwd Isaf Clun Gwyn

Cwm Porth

START 1

P

Afon Mellte

2

Sgwd Clun-Gwyn

2a

DANGER!
Very steep tree-root scramble
to narrow traverse ledge

Sgwd Isaf Clun-Gwyn

Return from here
to marker 25

Sgwd y Pannwr

0   Miles   ¼

Sgwd yr Eira

Afon Hepste

UPPER SYCHRYD WATERFALLS
via the Gunpowder works

DESCRIPTION Lovely woodland, pretty falls, mining history and industry make this a great 2½ mile walk. You will notice some wind-up audio boxes en-route telling the story of the works. Allow 1½ hours.

START From the car park at Craig y Dinas.

DIRECTIONS From the 'Heads of the Valleys' road – A465 – take the A4109 turn towards Glyn-nedd and Onllwyn. It is also signed to the National Show Caves complex of Dan yr Ogof. Continue to a cross roads and a set of traffic lights (the Dinas Hotel is seen on the opposite side of the road). Turn right here and 300 metres further on turn left on the B4242 signed to Pontneddfechan. Continue past The Angel to where there is a 'Y' junction, with the Dinas Inn to your right. Bear right and continue to where the road goes right and crosses the narrow bridge spanning the Afon Mellte. Turn left at the far side into the spacious car parking area. PLEASE DO NOT PARK IN THE VILLAGE.

I Turn right out of the car park and walk over the bridge. Take the turning on the right and then right again to pass by the side of the village vall. There is also a sign and an information board. Follow the wide track – the course of the tramway – and pass through a gate. Keep walking ahead ignoring left turns and pass in front of a white house. The track gradually becomes rougher. Ignore a right turning just past the house and continue ahead past an information board on your right to a barrier. Walk around this and continue to a bridge. DO NOT cross this but continue ahead. (Steps down to your right lead to a shelter). There are several small cascades on the next section which lead to another bridge spanning the Afon Mellte.

The remains of many buildings are seen to your left, part of the gunpowder works.

2 Cross the bridge and at the far side walk straight ahead and up a steep climb aided by steps to reach a finger post. DO NOT turn left here but go straight ahead on a level path. This begins to descend gradually to reach a fence and path junction. Go sharp left here and keep the fence to your right. At the next path junction take the obvious path down to your right where it descends steeply to reach a level platform overlooking the Afon Sychryd. The waterfalls are obvious – situated below a sturdy footbridge. At the far side of the bridge the large opening marks an abandoned Silica Mine. DO NOT ENTER.

3 Retrace your steps over the bridge and up the steep path to the junction with the sharp turn. Keeping the fence to your left walk straight ahead. This leads to a short section of wonderful soft grass before reaching the head of a rocky and steep incline. Follow this down to the car park. CARE is required in wet weather as the rock on the incline is very slippery.

Established in 1820 the works were famous as they were the only example of their kind in Wales. At one time 65 people, including 10 women, worked here. Originally owned by the Vale of Neath Powder Company the works changed ownership in 1862. Messrs Curtis & Harvey merged the works into Nobel's Explosives Company. This name existed until 1926 when the works became part of ICI. The gunpowder produced here was primarily for use in coal mines and quarries – including the slate mines and quarries of North Wales.

The site stretched for 2 miles along the Afon Mellte, covered some 180 acres and, importantly, was well away from the village. Water, the only source of energy, was supplied by two weirs and a series of leats (water channels). Work started at 07.30 and ended at 16.30. There was a plentiful supply of wood for making charcoal, a constituent of gunpowder. The ratios were saltpetre 75%, charcoal 15% and sulphur 10%. There was a good means of transport, as some of the gun-

On the Mellte

powder was shipped abroad. The finished product was transported via the Neath & Tennant Canal to Briton Ferry and on to the ships. Later a tramway was built to the Vale of Neath railway. Horses hauling the trams (or drams) were shod with copper shoes to prevent sparks.

In the main the ruined buildings have only three walls. The other wall was probably constructed from wood, as was the roof, which would have blown off in an explosion (which occurred from time to time!).

The walls were whitewashed so that accumulations of gunpowder could be seen. On December 31st 1931 the works closed when the Home Office took black powder off the Permitted List of Explosives. The buildings were set on fire and demolished in 1932.

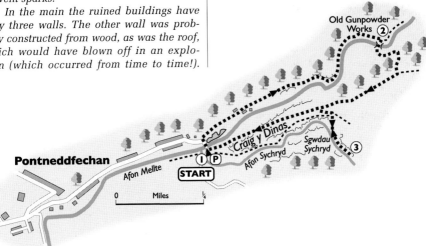

ABERDULAIS FALLS
All ability

DESCRIPTION Although not a long walk – just a few hundred metres – this is an interesting place to visit. Aberdulais Falls are very powerful after heavy rain and the remains of the associated ancient tin works are well worth a visit. The whole site is wheelchair friendly with ramps and lifts to offer the experience to all. A fee is payable to the National Trust who look after the area.

START From the Visitor Centre at Aberdulais Falls.

DIRECTIONS From the A465 'Heads of the Valleys' road take the A4109 turn signed to Blaendulais and Seven Sisters. Go round the roundabout to the A4109 and drive towards Blaendulais some 400 metres to the pull in on the left or the car park, on the opposite side of the road. Park your car in either of these places.

F rom the Visitor Centre the exhibits are obvious, as are the waterfalls, and you are left to explore the site for as long as you wish.

T he site has been utilised since 1584 due to the abundant supply of water for powering machinery. Initially copper was smelted here until around 1603. A Fulling and Tucking Mill was built on the site between around 1631. Tucking or Fulling is the process used to clean and thicken woollen cloth. A grist (corn/flour) mill was added during the period 1715 to 1720. It is also believed that iron working was carried on here between 1825 and 1830.

The tinplate period for which the area was chiefly known was between 1831 and 1877 at the upper site, ending in 1939 at the lower site. Nothing remains of this site. The upper site subsequently fell into ruin and become heavily overgrown. At one time there were some 225 tin mills in Britain with an astonishing 205 of these situated in South Wales. In 1842 a report from the Children's Commission revealed that there were 138 people working at both the upper and lower sites. Out those 138 people 34 were children aged between 8 and 13!

Unfortunately the old village of Aberdulais was largely destroyed by the construction of the A465, with the Dulais Rock Inn being the only building remaining from the original village.

Information boards along the way give you full details about each building. You can also obtain information from the Visitor Centre.

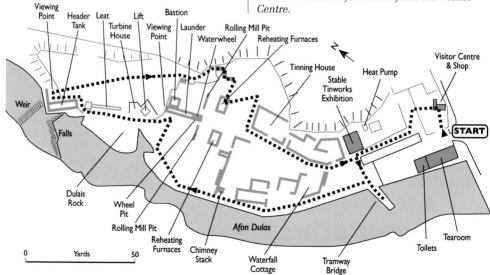

22

WALK 13

MELINCOURT WATERFALL

DESCRIPTION This easy 1¼ mile walk works well as an evening stroll or a short afternoon saunter. The path up the pretty, steep sided gorge is well maintained. The Melincourt Brook has many small attractive cascades, including one of 2 metres below the road bridge, above the 25 metres high waterfall. Allow an hour.

START At the car park designated for the reserve.

DIRECTIONS Approaching from the Merthyr Tydfil direction on the A465 'Heads of the Valleys' road, turn left into Resolven on the B4434. Follow the road into the village, go around a sweeping right hand bend and continue driving, passing St David's Church on your right, to the car park and picnic area on your right. Marion Hall, the pensioner's hall, is on your left.

2 Walk back down the path to a small flight of steps on your left. You will have noticed these on your walk up. Climb up these and follow the well marked path which curves round to the left and continues to a gate. Pass through this and continue along the level path to another gate. Go through this to join a very minor road. Turn left down this and across the bridge. Below this there is a fine cascade in Melincourt Brook. Continue down the road, ignoring a right turn, to a stile on your left. Here it is possible to climb over this to visit the ruins of the ironworks, but the path has become very overgrown. Continue down the steep road to the B4434. Turn left back to your car.

*J**M Turner**, a very notable artist, visited the area in 1795 and made a drawing of the waterfall which was included in his South Wales Sketchbook. It is now part of the Tate Gallery collection in London.*

Some years later Thomas Hornor came and produced a painting of the fall and ironworks. This clearly showed the large overshot waterwheel used for the blast furnace.

Melincourt ironworks started production in 1708 relying on charcoal for fuel. Water was also used as a source of energy. The large overshot waterwheel, powered by a diverted watercourse, drove the air bellows. Unfortunately nothing remains of this waterwheel.

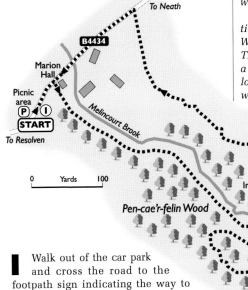

I Walk out of the car park and cross the road to the footpath sign indicating the way to the waterfall. Follow this well maintained path for 500 metres to the viewing area close to the waterfall. Either return to your car or –

23

WALK 14

AFON NEDD & SGWD CLUN GWYN

DESCRIPTION Lovely woodland, attractive rivers and a superb waterfall make this a lovely 4¼ mile walk. Allow 3½ hours.

START At Pont Melin Fach.

DIRECTIONS From the 'Heads of the Valleys' road – A465 – take the A4109 turn towards Glyn-nedd and Onllwyn. It is also signed to the National Show Caves complex of Dan yr Ogof. Continue to a cross roads and a set of traffic lights (the Dinas Hotel is seen on the opposite side of the road). Turn right here and 300 metres further on turn left on the B4242 signed to Pontneddfechan. Continue past The Angel to a 'Y' road junction (the Dinas Inn is on your right). Go left up the hill and around a steep bend. Continue through the village. Keep driving gradually uphill to where the road levels just past the well signed Gwern Blaedda farm. Turn left down a narrow road where a sign indicates that the road is not suitable for coaches! Follow this road down to the picnic site by the bridge.

1 From the car park walk back over the bridge and climb over the stile on your left. Climb up the muddy bank on your right for 40 metres and bear left on a fairly obvious path. This continues above the Afon Nedd and small cliffs. (Alternatively in low water conditions follow the path along the waters edge using stepping stones as required to where the path goes up a steep bank. Turn sharp right and then sharp left along the cliff top. There is a waterfall in wet weather on the far bank). Continue on the high level path with fine cascades in the river below. Descend gradually to the river and then back up to a stile. Cross this and continue to another. Continue straight ahead to Pont Rhyd-y-Cnau which spans the Afon Nedd to your left.

2 Turn right up the wide rough track towards Gwaun Bryn Bwch and continue to a gate. Go through this and keep following the track gradually up to another gate. Go through this to join a narrow tarmac road. Turn right and follow the road to a 'T' junction. Turn left and then right 20 metres further. Go through a gate where there is sign indicating the way to Porth yr Ogof. Walk down the track to a marker post and gate on your left. Go through the gate and walk down the obvious path through three more gates to a gate just before the road. Go through this and turn right to Cwm Porth. There are toilets and an Information Centre here. (Porth yr Ogof is close by).

3 From the car park cross back over the road and follow the concrete causeway path between two entrances into the cave below. Follow the sign indicating the way to Blue Pool and Waterfalls. Pass through a kissing gate and follow the river downstream to a footbridge. Cross this and at the far side turn left to follow the well marked path up to a viewing area for Sgwd Clun Gwyn. Continue along the very well marked path to a fence corner and walk up to your right. Continue to a finger post. Walk straight ahead – signed for the car park. Follow the level path to a kissing gate. Go through this and along the track to a track junction. Go left and down to a kissing gate left of a cattle grid. Pass through the gate and walk up to the road.

4 Turn right along the road to a small shop and petrol station. Continue past the shop for 50 metres and climb over a stile on your left to enter a field – indicated by a finger post. Walk across the field, heading slightly rightwards to a marker post. Bear right to a stile to the right of a gate. Climb over and walk half right keeping a fence to your left and a wall to your right, and go over another stile 50 metres further on. Go over this and head down a grassy track to a gate. Go through this and walk down a muddy path with a fence on your left and a low wall to your right. Continue through two more gates. Turn right down a sunken track. This bears left by a gate on your right. Keep following the sunken track to a stile left of a gate. Climb over this and walk down a short access road to the narrow road. Turn right down this back to your car.

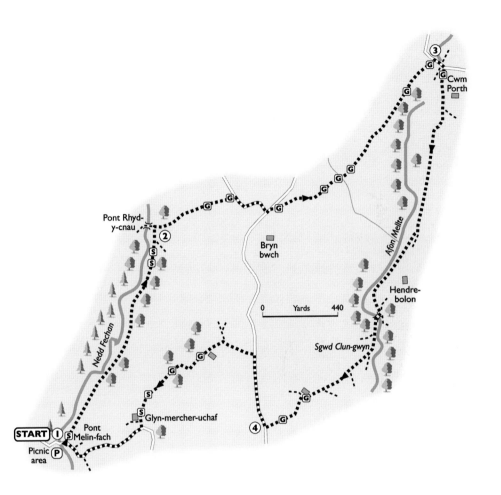

Before setting off for your walk a visit to see Porth yr Ogof is 'essential'. Walk with care down the slippery path to a seat at the bottom. To your left are twin stiles. Climb over either one down to the river's edge. Walk along a flat platform a few metres to its end. It is unwise to go further due to falling debris. The entrance is the largest in Wales at 15 metres wide and 4 metres high. The river on your right is not the real river however. It is only an overflow from the main flow that flows year round through the Tradesman's Entrance. This is seen by going to the right from the seat. The river known as the Afon Mellte means 'lightning river'. It rises incredibly quickly during rainfall and goes down equally quickly. There are 15 entrances into the system. Although used by many Outdoor Centres the cave has claimed the lives of 11 people.

PONTSTICIL RESERVOIR CIRCULAR

DESCRIPTION Starting by the reservoir this 6 mile walk climbs steadily above it before descending to the village of Pontsticil. At the high point there are tremendous views of the Brecon Beacons and the reservoir on this little-travelled walk. From the village the walk continues along the Taff Trail. In the summer months the cheery sound of the Brecon Mountain Railway is heard as it chuffs along the lake side. Allow 3 hours.

START From the car parking area on the left of the dead end road 200 metres past the road junction. This is just before crossing the bridge between Pontsticil Reservoir and Pentwyn Reservoir.

DIRECTIONS From Brecon take the A470 towards Merthyr Tydfil. Turn left into Cefn Coed y Cymer on the A4054. Turn left immediately before crossing over the 'Heads of the Valleys' (A465) road towards Pontsticil and Tal-y-Bont on Usk. Drive through Pontsticil and at a 'Y' junction bear left towards Tal-y-Bont. Continue along the west side of Pontsticil reservoir to a road junction. Go right along the dead end road for 200 metres to the car parking area on your left.

1 Walk along the road from your car and over the bridge. Continue up the road to a railway bridge. Immediately before this, walk steeply down the path, signed as a bridleway, to the lake shore. Cross over the top of the stone retaining wall to the far side and go up the path to the railway line. Follow the path alongside the line with a fence to your left to where it becomes a track just after the sailing club. Continue along the track to another coming up from your right.

2 Immediately before this turn left under the railway bridge – indicated by a marker post. Go steeply up bearing right at a path junction. Continue with great views of the Brecon Beacons opening up behind you. The path continues up to a gate. Walk through this and bear half right across the slope, where the path has disappeared! Keep 100 metres or so above the forest below you and continue on that line to find the start of a path. Follow this, again on the same line, across a boggy patch to reach a stream. Descend to it and cross over. Follow a narrow path on the far side to another stream spanned by an old railway sleeper.

3 Cross this and walk half left to where some fence posts are silhouetted against the sky. Walk towards these. Follow the fence above the small quarry below, followed by a wall. *There are marvellous views of the Brecon Beacons and the reservoir from here.* Follow the wall to where it descends into a large old quarry. Walk around the top edge of the quarry with care to pick up a path. Follow this to a gate seen to your right. DO NOT go through this but continue to a wooden post and gate below. These are directly above the dam. The gate has a dark blue topped lever. Walk through the gate and follow the path diagonally across the hill side, at first following the line of a ruined wall, to a fence. Keep the fence to your right and follow the path down to a gate. Go through this by the marker post and following the direction indicated continue down under the railway. Go through a gate at the far end to join a track. Cross over this and continue to another gate and then down to a finger post. Go through the gate here to join the road.

4 Turn left and walk down to your right into the water treatment works road. Turn left through some posts to join a road. Turn right and walk up the steep road into the village. At a 'T' junction turn right. If it is lunch time you may wish to have your lunch in the Red Cow pub, on your left, before continuing. Walk along the road to a 'Y' junction and bear left towards Tal-y-Bont. Walk past the new treatment works to the Taf Fechan and Taff Trail signs on your left. Turn left here to follow the forest track to where it ends at a picnic table. A tarmac path continues down to a footbridge across a

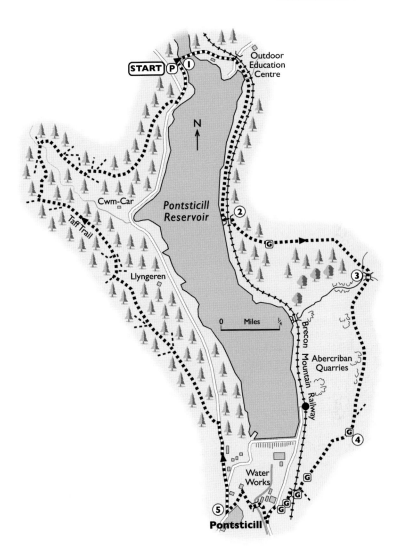

deep ravine. Cross over and follow the path up to join a track. Follow this to a 'T' junction. Turn left here – signed for the Taff Trail.

Follow this all the way to the road. Turn left. At the road junction go right along the dead end road back to your car.

LLYN CWM LLWCH

DESCRIPTION This 6 mile walk to the summit of Pen y Fan can easily be shortened for those who just want to visit the very pretty lake and the Tommy Jones memorial. The views from Pen y Fan are outstanding. NOTE – Corn Du and Pen y Fan are high mountain tops. In fact Pen y Fan is the highest mountain in Britain south of Snowdonia! Ensure that you are well prepared for mist and rapid changes of weather. Allow 4¼ hours.

START From the parking area at the end of the road.

DIRECTIONS At the western end of the start of the A40 dual carriageway turn left into Brecon. Opposite the Drovers Arms and just before the Renault Garage turn right into Ffrwdgrech Road. Keep going straight up this road to an obvious three pronged junction. Follow the middle road and keep going until you reach a cross roads. Go straight across and drive to gate at the end of the tarmac road. Go through this into the grassy parking area.

I Walk along the track by the side of the tumbling Nant Cwm Llwch to a footbridge. Cross this and go over a stile left of a gate. Keep following the track to a marker post on your right. (This is just before a gate leading into the property of Cwm Llwch Cottage). Go right here and then bear left to another marker post. Keeping the wall to your left continue to a stile. Climb over this and bear left to another. Cross this and follow the grassy track uphill, gradually at first. The track becomes steeper as a fence is reached. Climb over the stile. (From here it is possible to go left making a short detour to visit a small but picturesque waterfall). From the stile keep walking uphill to a cairn. The main path goes right at this point but you bear left. Follow this path to a final short steep pull to Llyn Cwm Llwch, which remains hidden until the very last moment. If desired the walk can be ended here and a return made back to your car.

2 To the right of some large sandstone blocks, close to the lake edge, a faint path goes up a short spur. As height is gained the path becomes more pronounced but steeper. Keep walking up to join the ridge with superb views down to the lake. Continue up to the Tommy Jones memorial. (If you do not wish to ascend to the summit then this is the place to turn around and continue down the broad ridge of Pen Milan – see paragraph **3**). Keep walking up the ridge on a very well worn path to the summit of Corn Du at 873 metres. Pen y Fan 886 metres is reached ¼ mile further and the way is obvious – in fine weather. *There are magnificent views from Pen y Fan.* When you have had enough of these retrace your steps to Corn Du and the Tommy Jones memorial.

3 From here return down the ridge you previously walked along for 150 metres to where you emerged on to the ridge on your outward walk on the path from Cwm Llwch. Do not descend here but continue down very gradually around the head of the escarpment on a narrow but well trodden path, around a broad grassy nose. Follow the continuation of the narrow path to where it joins a wider grassy track. Turn right and continue down Pen Milan. The track switchbacks first right then left before descending gradually to where it tries to lose itself at a patch of gorse. Keep on the intermittent track, trending towards a white walled cottage. Go left when a fence is reached and descend to the bottom of the field where there is a stile and a gate. There is also a National Trust sign indicating Pen Milan. Cross the stile to reach a green lane. Continue down this for 100 metres to a cottage. There is a finger post across the tiny stream to your right. Cross the stream and climb over the stile by the finger post. Follow the left edge of the field to another stile. Go over this and walk slightly right and up to another stile at the top edge of the field. Cross this and walk to the boundary wall of the cottage, where here is a marker. When the wall bends right, walk across the field to reach a third stile at the field corner. Climb over this and continue to your car.

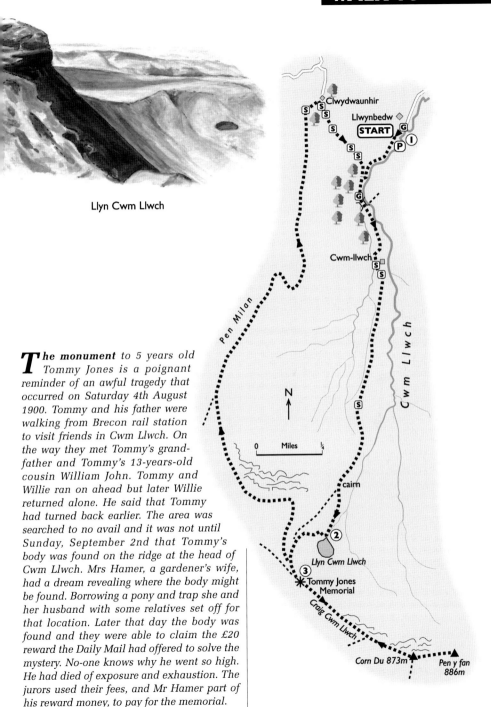

Llyn Cwm Llwch

*T*he monument to 5 years old Tommy Jones is a poignant reminder of an awful tragedy that occurred on Saturday 4th August 1900. Tommy and his father were walking from Brecon rail station to visit friends in Cwm Llwch. On the way they met Tommy's grandfather and Tommy's 13-years-old cousin William John. Tommy and Willie ran on ahead but later Willie returned alone. He said that Tommy had turned back earlier. The area was searched to no avail and it was not until Sunday, September 2nd that Tommy's body was found on the ridge at the head of Cwm Llwch. Mrs Hamer, a gardener's wife, had a dream revealing where the body might be found. Borrowing a pony and trap she and her husband with some relatives set off for that location. Later that day the body was found and they were able to claim the £20 reward the Daily Mail had offered to solve the mystery. No-one knows why he went so high. He had died of exposure and exhaustion. The jurors used their fees, and Mr Hamer part of his reward money, to pay for the memorial.

29

LLYN SYFADDAN

Llangors Lake

DESCRIPTION This easy and gentle 3½ mile walk is good as an evening stroll or for a short afternoon. Llangors Lake, as it is usually known, is the largest natural stretch of inland water in South Wales. Unfortunately access for walkers is very limited. Although there is a short loop at the end of the outward leg it is essentially a there and back the same way walk! Fortunately, because of this general lack of access, natural life flourishes and the area is a wildlife sanctuary. The early part of the walk can be extremely swampy. Wearing Wellington boots will certainly keep your feet dry! Allow 1¾ hours.

START At the car park by the toilets on Llangors Common.

DIRECTIONS From Talgarth follow the B4560 for 4 miles towards Bwlch. Turn right into Llangors village and then turn right on the brow of a steep hill – signed 'To Lake'. Continue for 250 metres and turn left – again signed 'To Lake' – on to Llangors Common. Drive down to the large but rough car park by the public toilets on your left.

1 From the car park cross the road and walk across Llangorse Common on a grassy path, roughly midway between the caravan site and the sailing club building, to a footbridge over the Afon Llynfi. *Pen y Fan and Cribin make a wonderful backdrop to your right.* Go up some steps, cross the bridge and through the gate on the far side as waymarked. Walk half right to cross the centre of the field and pass through the kissing gate at the far side of the field. This section is extremely wet and swampy. Continue in the same direction passing a clump of reeds that successfully hide the lake from view! Go through the next kissing gate. Just beyond there are two very gnarly old oak trees. Pass through another gate to reach a footbridge.

2 Cross the bridge and go through the gate at the far end. Bear left and walk across more swampy ground and through another gate to a marker post at the edge of Llangasty Nature Reserve. Over to your left on the far side of the lake is the islet of Crannog, whilst up the field to your right is Tymawr Farm. This dates back to 1584. Go up to your right here on the edge of the field keeping the hedge on your right. A hidden stile on the right in this hedge is reached. Climb over this to reach a track. Cross over to another stile. Climb over this to enter the orchard and walk up the right-hand edge, again keeping the hedge to your right, to another stile. Climb over this and turn sharp left keeping the hedge to your left. Continue to a stile. Go over this to join a farm track and bear left then right at a marker post.

3 Walk along the farm track above the farm to a gate on your left. Pass through this and go right to a fence. Keeping this to your right continue to where it ends. Go up to a stile. Climb over this and walk across the next field, keeping the hedge to your right, to the next stile. Cross over this to meet a narrow road. Turn left down the road to pass the Llangasty Retreat, seen to your left. Just before the church of St Gastyn, Llangasty-Talyllyn is the Old School, a private residence since 1925. Continue to the small car park by the lake.

4 After admiring the lake, and the church, return to the finger post seen to your left when entering the small car park indicating the way back to Llangors. Go through the kissing gate and walk along the bottom edge of the field, with great views of the lake, to another kissing gate. Pass through this and, keeping the hedge to your right, continue across the field to yet another kissing gate. Pass through this and enter a small wood. Cross a footbridge to reach a kissing gate. Go through this and walk along a boardwalk. At the end of the boardwalk keep the fence to your right to a wide wooden farm gate. Go through this and bear left to a kissing gate to the left of another wide farm gate. Cross the field by the obvious path to a gate. Pass through this and walk across the field to where you turned up to your right on your outward walk. Retrace your steps back to your car.

*T*alyllyn *is a common Welsh word. It literally means 'end' or 'edge of the lake'. Llan, perhaps the most common prefix of place names in Wales, is often translated as church or parish. However, Llan was in use long before parishes existed. It means more correctly an enclosure or clearing in which there might have been a crude church and a few, even more crude, dwellings. The Welsh word for church is eglwys.*

The Crannog – an artificial island – may have been built to support a fortified palace and a few buildings. The remains were discovered in 1868. A legend was told by Giraldus Cambriensis, better known as Gerald of Wales, that a city lay hidden beneath the water of the lake. Gerald toured Wales looking for likely soldiers to fight in his crusades during the 12th century.

Another legend concerns a real prince who lived nearly 900 years ago. He was called Gruffudd ap Rhys and although no-one knows for

certain when he was born, he died in 1137. On one occasion he was travelling with Milo (Miles Fitzwalter), Earl of Hereford, Lord of Brecknock, Constable of England and Sheriff of Gloucester and Payn Fitzjohn, Lord of Ewyas. These last two noticed that the birds were unusually silent. Milo, who did not like Gruffudd, goaded him as to his roots. Gruffudd replied that he, unlike his friends, was a true Welshman and descended from Princes. Gruffudd threw down a challenge to both Milo and Payn that whoever was the true Prince of Wales could make the birds sing. Both Milo and Payn addressed the birds imploring them to sing. Although some flapped their wings or preened themselves the birds did not sing. When it was Gruffudd's turn he bade the birds to sing. Immediately all the birds burst into song, proving that Gruffudd was indeed a true Prince of Wales.

Another legend relates to a wicked princess who was so bad that her people and their city were destroyed under an avalanche of water. She was known as Princess Safaddon.

Finally, Llangasty-Talyllyn church is the only dedication to St Gastyn in the whole world! He preserved the Christian faith during the pagan invasion in the fifth and sixth centuries. Much more information is available if you make a small donation inside the church.

Llangorse Common

To Llangors

Lakeside Farm

START

Llangorse Sailing Club

N

crannog

Llangors Lake
Llyn Saffodyn

hide

Tymawr Farm

Llangasty-Talyllyn

Llan

0   Miles   ½

BLAEN-Y-GLYN WATERFALLS

DESCRIPTION This pleasant 2½ mile walk packs in many fine waterfalls and cascades. The lower part can often be busy but once away from this the walk enters peaceful surroundings as it heads into the eastern side of the Brecon Beacons. Allow 1¾ hours.

START At the Blaen-y-glyn car park beyond Talybont reservoir.

DIRECTIONS From Brecon take the A40 towards Abergavenny. Turn right at Llansantffraed towards Talybont-on-Usk. At the 'T' junction turn right on to the B4558 into the village. Drive past the Star Inn on your left. Immediately beyond the Post Office and stores on your right a steep turn left is taken to drive over the canal. Continue through the tiny hamlet of Aber and continue to Talybont reservoir. Drive past this until the signed car park is seen to your right. Park your car here.

I Walk out of the car park back to the road. Turn left and walk over the bridge spanning the Caerfanell. At the end of the bridge turn left over a stile. Follow the path alongside the river keeping it to your left to the first of the waterfalls. Go up a short steep path on your right and continue past more falls to a footbridge. The large waterfall seen ahead can be reached by paths on either side of the river. (For a short loop you can cross the footbridge and bear left to a stile. Cross this and walk up to a junction with a track. Turn left down the track and return to the car park).

2 Continue walking upstream keeping the river to your left. There are many falls and cataracts on this section. At a fence cross the stile and keep walking upstream – TAKE CARE on some narrow sections – to the last, but pretty waterfall. Continue another 30 metres to where the path crosses the river. *There are ivy clad trees on the far bank.* Cross the stream, which can at times be impassable. (If you

are unsure just retrace you steps back to the car park). The path continues and bears left above the ivy clad trees and away from the river to a stile immediately before a plantation). Cross the stile and follow a forest track to a major 'T' junction. Turn right here and walk down to a car park.

3 Just before reaching a cattle grid at the far end of the car park turn left down an obvious path. Follow this down passing by the first waterfall on the Nant Bwrefwr. Continue along the path to a junction. Turn right over two large fallen trees and walk down keeping the river to your right. There are several waterfalls of varying height on the way. Keep following the path down, high above the stream on your right. Continue to where the path becomes somewhat muddier and steeper. On your right here is the highest waterfall to be seen on the walk. At the bottom of the steep slope cross an inlet stream and continue down to a track. Turn right back to the car park.

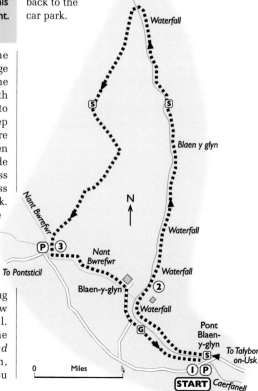

32

WALK 19

PWLL-Y-WRACH WATERFALL
Witches Pool

DESCRIPTION This is a very pretty but overlooked area. Beyond the waterfall the route continues through woodland before walking along a short section of road. This is followed by a descent through fine woodland. An interesting stepping stone crossing of the River Ennig is followed by more woodland walking before heading back to the car park. 2½ miles, 1½ hours.

START At the small car park for the Pwll-y-Wrach Nature Reserve.

DIRECTIONS From the square in the centre of Talgarth drive over the bridge by the Bridge Inn and turn sharp left. Go up to a 'Y' junction and fork left – signed to Pwll-y-Wrach. Continue up this road to the small car park on the right of the narrow road.

I Leave the car park through the gate by the obvious information sign and walk along the level ALL ABILITY trail. Where this ends – disappointingly not reaching the falls – go up and left and follow the often muddy path to the fine twin falls. The path continues up steps to the left of the waterfall to a stile. Cross this and continue straight ahead keeping the stream to your right. Ignore a sharp turn on the left and continue to a stile. Cross this and join a narrow road. Turn right along it and walk along to a bridge spanning the River Ennig. Cross the bridge – phone box to your left – and continue up the dead end road towards Troed-yr-harn farm. Just before reaching the farm buildings a stile on your left is seen.

2 Climb over this to enter a field. Keeping the fence to your right follow the right-hand edge of the field to a stile.

Cross this and another 30 metres further. Walk straight down the field to climb over another stile. Turn sharp right to yet another stile 50 metres further on. This is crossed to enter a wood. Walk down the path – there is a waterfall in the stream below and to your left – to a footbridge. Do not cross this but turn right and follow the path above the stream to a huge fallen log. Turn left here down some wooden steps to the stream bank. Follow the path alongside the stream to where the path veers away and climbs up to join a wide track. Cross this and follow the path down to a marker post. Ignore the arrows on this and continue straight ahead to join the River Ennig. Cross this via stepping stones – TAKING CARE – to a marker post. Walk left, downstream, to a marker post. Turn up to you right and continue to the next marker post and walk uphill to a gate on your left. Do not go through the gate but turn right and walk along the good path to a path junction. Turn sharp left and walk up steps back to your car.

*P*wll-y-Wrach *is an SSSI. As such you can find many ferns and flowers here. These flowers include Herb Bennet, which was regarded as one of the most powerful of natural charms. Black Bryony can also be found and although poisonous the berries were once used for curing bruises and chilblains. Wood Sorrel, flowering around Easter, is known locally as 'Alleluiah'. At night when the three petals close it is known as 'Sleeping Beauty'. The area around Pwll-y-Wrach has the most important colony of dormice in the area. Over 180 species of flowering plants have been recorded here.*

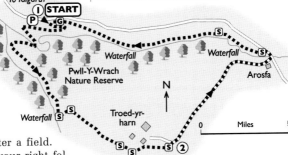

33

GRWYNE FAWR RESERVOIR

DESCRIPTION This 3½ mile walk initially follows the infant Grwyne Fawr river, which has many very pretty cataracts. The crossing of the dam allows wonderful views of the reservoir and of the Black Mountains. The walk back gives lovely views of the valley. Grwyne Fawr reservoir is the only such expanse of water in the Black Mountains! This walk allows for more strenuous options for those so minded. Allow 1¾ hours.

START At the Mynydd Du car park very close to the road end.

DIRECTIONS From Abergavenny follow the A465 towards Hereford and turn left at Llanfihangel Crucorney. Follow signs towards Cwmyoy and then turn left at a phone box towards Forest Coal Pit, Partrishow and Llanbedr. At the cross roads bear right. Pass by a phone box and the Mynydd Du sign on your right and continue to the large car park on your right.

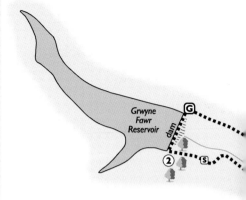

I Leave the car park and turn right and walk up the road to a gate. Go through this and another gate following the narrow road. Continue walking up the road with the river to your right, which has numerous pretty cataracts, to an obvious pull in for vehicles on the right. Opposite this, turn left and walk up just to the right of a stream to a fence. Follow this fence up to a stile. Go over this and continue to a small wood. At a small boulder and the first tree bear right to reach the left hand end of the dam.

2 Turn right to cross the dam. At the far end turn right and walk through a small avenue of conifers to a gate. Pass through a gap in the fence left of this and follow the track gradually down to a gate. Go through this and continue down to join the road back to your car.

There are more strenuous options. From the far side of the dam the walk can be continued, initially by the side of Grwyne Fawr and then following the stream up to the low point on the ridge. Here you can turn left to return over Waun Fach – the highest point on the Black Mountains – and Pen y Gadair Fawr to walk down to the edge of the forest to the car park. There is a footbridge to cross the Grwyne Fawr. OR you could turn right and climb Rhos Dirion and turn right to follow the path that leads along the opposite ridge to the Blacksmith's Anvil and follow the path from there down to the car park.

*A**lthough** the idea of building a reservoir had been mooted by Baldwin Latham in 1906 construction of the Grwyne Fawr Reservoir did not begin until 1912. Due to the war and construction difficulties it was not opened until March 1928. At the same time the 2 million gallon Cwmtillery service reservoir would be built along with the 1608 yards long Coity tunnel to carry the 16 inch water pipe into the valley. Construction started in 1912, being completed in 1915. The feed pipe runs from Grwyne Fawr to Llwyn Ddu Reservoir, Abergavenny, Clydach Gorge and Llanelly Hill. It turns right at the Whistle Inn and on through the Coity Tunnel to emerge at Blaentillery Farm and terminates at the top Cwmtillery Reservoir.*

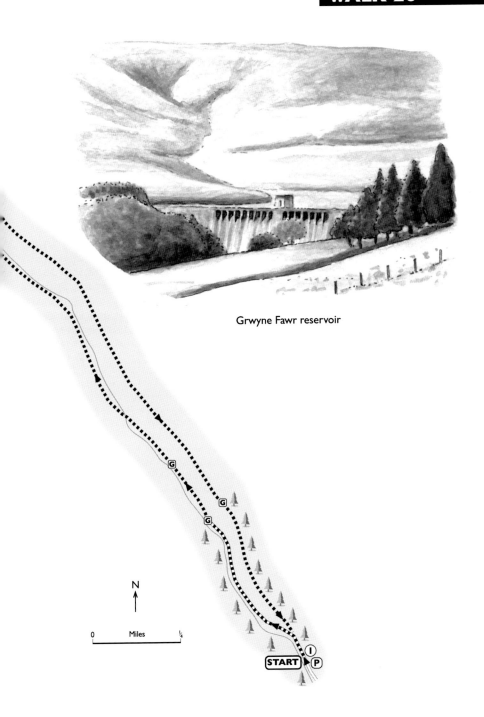

Grwyne Fawr reservoir

N
↑

0   Miles   ¼

START ▶ Ⓘ Ⓟ

THE GREAT BIG WATERFALLS WALK

DESCRIPTION This 10 mile walk links many waterfalls in one big outing. The falls are – Sgwd Gwladus, Sgwd y Bedol (Horseshoe Falls), Sgwd Ddwli Isaf, Sgwd Ddwli Uchaf, Sgwd Clun Gwyn, Sgwd y Pannwr, Sgwd Isaf Clun Gwyn, Sgwd yr Eira and the Upper Sychryd Falls. Allow 6 hours.

START At a small car park close to The Angel pub in Pontneddfechan.

DIRECTIONS From the 'Heads of the Valleys' road – A465 – take the A4109 turn towards Glyn-nedd and Onllwyn. It is also signed to the National Show Caves complex of Dan yr Ogof. Continue to a cross roads and a set of traffic lights. (The Dinas Hotel is seen on the opposite side of the road). Turn right here and, 300 metres further on, turn left on the B4242 signed to Pontneddfechan. Continue to The Angel where there is parking close by. DO NOT park in the car park belonging to the pub.

1 From the car park walk through the metal gate with Sgwd Gwladus clearly marked. Follow the good path to a gate and stile. Take your pick which you use! Continue following the track. There is evidence of mining along this section, as is seen by the blocked off adits. Continue to a footbridge. Do not cross this but continue up with the Afon Pyrddin to your right. A viewing area is reached where Sgwd Gwladus is clearly seen. Return to the bridge and cross over. Follow the Pyrddin upstream for an alternative view of the fall and return to the bridge.

2 Do not cross but walk ahead to join the Afon Nedd Fechan and follow this delightful river upstream. The path rises to high above the river but then gradually descends back to it again to cross a footbridge. Continue to the next footbridge where on the right is the lovely and well named Sgwd y Bedol (Horseshoe Falls). Continue upstream to above Sgwd Ddwli Isaf and another foot-

bridge. Cross this and continue upstream to the next very pretty fall Sgwd Ddwli Uchaf. Here the approach to the bottom of the fall is via an easy path that leads off from the main path some 200 metres before the waterfall. Return to the main path and continue up to a picnic site at Pont Melin Fach.

3 From the car park walk over the bridge and climb the stile on your left. Climb up the muddy bank on your right for 40 metres and bear left on a fairly obvious path. This continues above the Afon Nedd and small cliffs. (Alternatively in low water conditions it is better to follow the path along the water's edge using stepping stones as required to where the path goes up a steep bank. Turn sharp right and then sharp left along cliff top. There is a waterfall in wet weather on the far bank). Continue on the high level path with fine cascades in the river below. Descend gradually to the river and then back up to a stile. Cross this and continue to another. Continue straight ahead to Pont Rhyd-y-Cnau, which spans the Afon Nedd to your left.

4 Turn right towards Gwaun Bryn Bwch up the wide rough track and continue to a gate. Go through this and keep following the track gradually up to another gate. Go through this to join a narrow tarmac road. Turn right and follow the road to a 'T' junction. Turn left and then right 20 metres further. Go through a gate where there is sign indicating the way to Porth yr Ogof. Walk down the track to a marker post and gate on your left. Go through the gate and walk down the obvious path through three more gates to a gate just before the road. Go through this and turn right to Cwm Porth. There are toilets and an information centre here. (It is an easy matter to visit Porth yr Ogof from the car park).

5 Cross the road from the car park and take the path that follows a short length of concrete causeway between two cave entrances. These lead into the Porth yr Ogof system. Bear left and follow the sign towards Blue Pool and Waterfalls. Go through a kissing gate and follow the path alongside the Afon Mellte to a footbridge. Walk past the bridge and continue on the main path up past a small section of fence on your left. Keep walking to join a fence to your right and continue to a finger post. Descend here to admire Sgwd Clun Gwyn.

6 Return to the finger post and follow the red indicator towards Sgwd yr Eira. Markers numbered 16 – 25 are followed to another finger post. To reach Sgwd yr Eira, continue o the next finger post – number 3 – pointing the way down to it. Follow the path down via some steps to the fall. Walk around the back of this and follow the steep path up the far side to a finger post.

7 Turn right towards Craig y Dinas. Continue along this path, which can be very wet at times, to some ruins. Bear right and down passing marker posts before bearing left along the main path. Keep going to a fence and a gate. Go through this keeping on the path to a finger post indicating the way to the Gunpowder Works. Ignore this and continue ahead to a fence. Turn left and walk to where the path bends to the right with another going straight ahead. Bear right down where it descends steeply to reach a level platform overlooking the Afon Sychryd. The waterfalls are obvious, situated below a sturdy footbridge. At the far side of the bridge the large opening enters an abandoned Silica Mine. DO NOT ENTER.

8 Retrace your steps over the bridge and up the steep path to the junction with the sharp turn. Keeping the fence to your left walk straight ahead. This leads to a short section of wonderful soft grass before reaching the head of a rocky and steep incline. Follow this down to the car park. *CARE is required in wet weather as the rock on the incline is very slippery.* Leave the car park and cross the bridge. Turn left and walk through the village to a road junction. Continue straight ahead back to your car – or The Angel for drink or three – you have earned it!

Porth yr Ogof

Cwm Porth

Afon Mellte

Afon Nedd Fechan

Sgwd Clun-Gwyn

Sgwd Isaf Clun-Gwyn

Pont Melin-fach

Sgwd y Pannwr

Sgwd yr Eira

Nedd Hepste

Sgwd Ddwli Uchaf

Sgwd Ddwli Isaf

N

Sgwd Gwladus

Horseshoe Falls
Sgwd y Bedol

Pontneddfechan

Craig y Dinas

Sgwdau Sychryd

Afon Sychryd

A465

Waterfall
START

0   Miles   ½

CWM RHAEADR

DESCRIPTION A pretty 3 mile walk in mixed deciduous and coniferous woodland that has an adventurous finale for those who want a little more spice in their walk. The waterfalls are situated in very dramatic surroundings. If sticking to the main route the walk is only 2½ miles. Allow 2 hours or 1½ hours for the regular walk. The walk is well signed with blue markers – apart from the section up to the falls.

START From the Cwm Rhaeadr Forestry Commission car park.

DIRECTIONS Follow the A483 from Llandovery towards Builth Wells for 400 metres to a zebra crossing. Turn left here. Follow the minor road under a railway bridge and continue for just over 2½ miles to a left turn signed to Cil-y-Cwm. Drive through the village to a sign on your right indicating the car park to Cwm Rhaeadr is 50 metres further. Turn left into this car park and park in the lower of the two parks. There is an information board here.

I Walk out of the car park by a finger post and a blue marker post up the path and continue to a path junction. There is a marker post here marked 39. Go straight ahead here and continue to a track. Just before this on your right is a fine wooden carving of a horse. There is an information board at this junction. Cross the track half-left to a marker post and continue up to the next junction and turn right. At the next junction walk down the left hand path firstly down then up past a seat on your right – close to a path junction. Walk up to your right. The path levels and continues along past two seats. It then descends slightly to a junction. Go up to your right here – marker post 48 – to another path junction marker post (38). Go left along the path to where it descends to a junction with a track – marker post 45. Walk left and follow the track down to marker post 66 on the left at the junction. Turn right here along the track. Just after a huge pipe swallowing the stream a stile is seen to your right.

2 For those who do not wish to go up to the falls miss this section and go to no. **3**. For the adventurous the walk up to the falls is well worthwhile. Whilst not difficult the path is exposed in places, narrow and has a tricky, slippery, crossing of the stream. *This alternative will be impossible after heavy rain.* Go over the stile and walk up, keeping close to the fence on your left. At the fence corner turn right and follow the path to where it descends to the stream. Cross this slippery obstacle carefully to the far side. Continue up the narrow but not very steep path to the base of the falls. It's an impressive spot. Retrace your steps back to the stile. Instead of climbing back up to the fence corner, follow the path alongside the stream back to the stile and the track where you turn right it. Follow the directions as in **3** below.

3 Continue walking along the track for another 70 metres to marker post 91. Turn left down a grassy track. Keep following the path, which becomes a track, passing several marker posts and, keeping the stream to your left. Keep walking down to a footbridge. Cross this and walk up to a track. Turn right along this to where the track bends to your right at a prominent junction with a path at marker post 29. Go up the quite steep path to marker post 39 seen earlier and turn right back to the car park.

An all ability and barrier-free trail goes off from the higher car park. Go up and left out of the car park and go up to a junction. Turn right to follow the gravely track in an anti clockwise direction around for ¾ mile. It passes two pretty ponds and several picnic places. *Allow 30 minutes for this.*

The sculpture of the horse traditionally commemorates Henry Tudor, who rode a horse bred in this area to the Battle of Bosworth, where he won the crown of England.

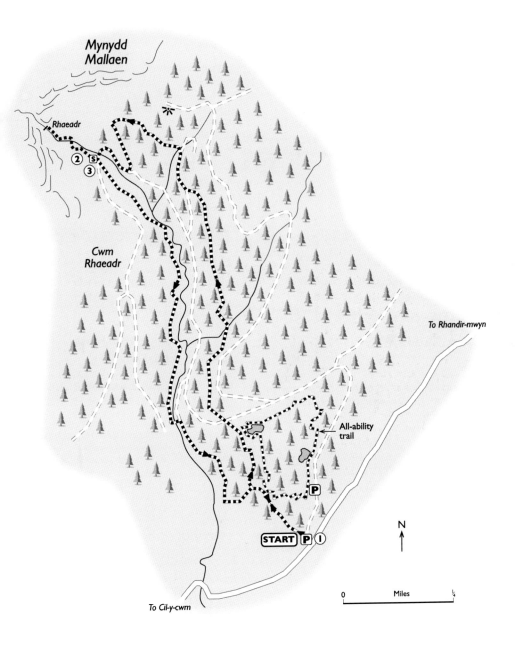

Mynydd
Mallaen

Rhaeadr

② Ⓢ
③

Cwm
Rhaeadr

To Rhandir-mwyn

All-ability
trail

P

START P ①

To Cil-y-cwm

N

0   Miles   ¼

PRONUNCIATION

These basic points should help non-Welsh speakers

Welsh	English equivalent
c	always hard, as in cat
ch	as on the Scottish word loch
dd	as 'th' in then
f	as 'f in of
ff	as 'ff in off
g	always hard as in got
ll	no real equivalent. It is like 'th' in then, but with an 'L' sound added to it, giving 'thlan' for the pronunciation of the Welsh 'llan'.

In Welsh the accent usually falls on the last-but-one syllable of a word.

KEY TO THE MAPS

————	Main road
————	Minor road
•→•→	Walk route and direction
①	Walk instruction
– – –	Path
⌒⌣	River/stream
Ⓖ	Gate
Ⓢ	Stile
△	Summit
🌲🌳	Woods
▼	Pub
Ⓟ	Parking

THE COUNTRYSIDE CODE

• Be safe – plan ahead and follow any signs

• Leave gates and property as you find them

• Protect plants and animals, and take your litter home

• Keep dogs under close control

• Consider other people

The CroW Act 2000, implemented throughout Wales in May 2005, introduced new legal rights of access for walkers to designated open country, predominantly mountain, moor, heath or down, plus all registered common land. This access can be subject to restrictions and closure for land management or safety reasons for up to 28 days a year.

Published by
Kittiwake Books Limited
3 Glantwymyn Village Workshops, Glantwymyn, Machynlleth, Montgomeryshire SY20 8LY

© Text & map research: Des Marshall 2011
© Maps & illustrations: Kittiwake 2011
Drawings: Morag Perrott
Cover photos: *Main* – Llangorse Lake. *Inset* – The lower part of Sgwd Isaf Clun Gwyn. Des Marshall.

Care has been taken to be accurate.
However neither the author nor the publisher can accept responsibility for any errors which may appear, or their consequences. If you are in any doubt about access, check before you proceed.

Printed by Mixam, UK.

ISBN: **978 1902302 87 4**